ICE WRECK

by Lucille Recht Penner
illustrated by David LaFleur

To Jonathan
L.P.

To David and Ruth,
for your unwavering love and support.
D.L.

Photo credits: pp. 7, 11, 28, and 42–43, Royal Geographical Society, London.

Library of Congress Cataloging-in-Publication Data
Penner, Lucille Recht.
Ice wreck / by Lucille Recht Penner ; illustrated by David LaFleur.
    p.   cm. — (Road to reading. Mile 4)
ISBN 0-307-26408-4 (pbk.) — ISBN 0-307-46408-3 (GB)
1. Shackleton, Ernest Henry, Sir, 1874–1922—Journeys—Juvenile literature.
2. Endurance (Ship)—Juvenile literature. 3. Imperial Trans-Antarctic
Expedition (1914–1917)—Juvenile literature. [1. Shackleton, Ernest Henry,
Sir, 1874–1922—Journeys. 2. Explorers. 3. Survival. 4. Endurance (Ship).
5. Imperial Trans-Antarctic Expedition (1914–1917). 6. Antarctica—
Discovery and exploration.] I. LaFleur, David. II. Title. III. Series.

G850 1914.S53 P46 2001
919.8'904—dc21   00-057671

A GOLDEN BOOK · **New York**
Golden Books Publishing Company, Inc.
New York, New York 10106

ISBN: 0-307-26408-4 (pbk)
ISBN: 0-307-46408-3 (GB)

10   9   8   7   6   5   4   3   2   1

CONTENTS

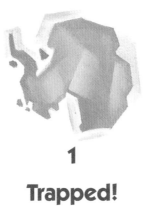

1

Trapped!

It was August 1914. Sir Ernest Shackleton stood in the bow of his sturdy wooden ship, the *Endurance*. Twenty-seven men and sixty-nine sled dogs were on board. The ship was headed for Antarctica.

Antarctica is a continent at the bottom of the world. It is the coldest place on Earth. No plants grow there. Few animals live there. In 1914, the only people who had ever been there were explorers.

So why did Shackleton want to go to Antarctica?

Shackleton was an explorer, too. He wanted to set a record—he wanted to be the first person to cross Antarctica from one side to the other. But that plan was in trouble.

Big chunks of ice filled the sea. Each day the ice grew thicker. The *Endurance* picked its way carefully. Ice is dangerous. It can tear a hole in a ship.

Then the temperature dropped. Ice froze around the ship. The *Endurance* couldn't go forward. It couldn't turn and go back. The men tried to break a path in the ice. And Shackleton did not give up. He gave new orders.

Raise the sails! Fire up the engines!
The *Endurance* charged at full speed
into the ice.

The ship couldn't break free. Soon it
couldn't move at all. Shackleton and
his men were trapped.

2

Abandon Ship!

The men looked out at the sea of ice. They couldn't cross Antarctica. They couldn't even get there. What would happen to them now?

Shackleton told them he had a new plan. They would live on the *Endurance* until the ice broke up. The ship was stocked with food. If they wanted fresh meat, they could hunt for seals and penguins. Then, when the ship was free, they would sail home.

But Shackleton knew the months ahead would not be easy. He ordered the ship's carpenter to build rooms in the warmest part of the ship.

Even the dogs got new homes, built out of ice blocks. The crew called the little houses dogloos.

The dogs were fun. The men played with them and treated them like pets. When a dog named Sally had puppies, Tom Crean, the second officer, built a tiny sled for the puppies to pull.

Some of the men went hunting
for seals. The ship's captain, Frank
Worsley, scrambled up the sails' ropes.
Worsley had great eyesight. If he saw a
seal, he signaled to the men below and
they hurried after it.

But often there was nothing to do.

The men were bored. Shackleton tried to cheer them up. He taught them card games. He recited poetry. He was kind to everyone.

The men came to love him. They called him Boss. The Boss started singing contests, debates, slide shows,

and guessing games. One night, the crew dressed up in fancy costumes and put on a skit.

Outside they played wild games of ice soccer and hockey. They held a race with their dog teams and called it the Great Antarctic Dog Derby. The men yelled and cheered as the dogs thundered over the ice.

But soon they began to worry again. They had been trapped by the ice for seven months and the ship was still stuck. Now the weather was getting worse.

A fierce storm blew up. The men

heard the ice grinding and groaning nearby. Sheets of ice pressed together so hard that they pushed each other up in the air.

"The ship can't live in this, Skipper," Shackleton told Frank Worsley. "It is only a matter of time. . . . What the ice gets, the ice keeps."

He was right. Ice squeezed the *Endurance* tighter and tighter. One terrifying day, the ship rolled onto its side. A few hours later, it rolled back. The men didn't feel safe anymore.

All around them, the ice rocked and trembled. The *Endurance* sprang leaks.

Everyone worked to pump out the water. Some of the men jumped over the side and hacked at the ice with shovels and axes. But it was no use. The ice was too thick to scrape away.

Then a huge piece of ice ripped a hole in the side of the ship. Water poured in. The *Endurance* was breaking up. Soon it was going to sink.

Sadly, Shackleton gave the order. *Abandon ship*.

3

Onto the Ice

The little band of men stood on the
wet ice. Boxes and bags were heaped
at their feet. Shackleton had made
sure that food, supplies, tents, sleds,
and lifeboats were saved from the
Endurance. They set up camp.

Wind howled over the ice. The men
were scared. Shackleton was worried,

too, but he didn't show it. He acted calm and cheerful. "Ship and stores have gone," he said. "So now we'll go home."

He had already made another plan. They would cross the ice to open water. Then they would get in the

lifeboats and sail to a place called
Paulet's Island. It wasn't far, and lots of
supplies were stored there.

The Boss gave out sleeping bags
made of reindeer skin. But there were
only eighteen of them. Some of the
men would have to use plain blankets.
Shackleton held a lottery for the warm
bags. He didn't take part in it. He took
only a blanket for himself. He even gave
away his thick boots to a man whose
own boots were ragged and torn.

The men loaded up the lifeboats
and sleds. When Shackleton gave the
order, they started across the ice. The

dogs pulled the sleds. The men
dragged the lifeboats.

But it was hard to walk on the
jagged ice. The men and the dogs
stumbled and fell again and again. At
the end of the day, they had covered

less than two miles. And everyone was exhausted.

The Boss saw that his plan wouldn't work. So he gave new orders. They would set up camp on a large sheet of floating ice called a floe. If they were

lucky, wind and ocean currents would carry them close to Paulet's Island.

They weren't lucky. Five months later, they were still camped on the ice. And they were drifting *away* from Paulet's Island.

The food was running out. Some of the men were weak from hunger. One sad day, there wasn't enough left to feed the dogs. Soon they would starve. The men had to shoot them. It was horrible. Frank Hurley, the ship's photographer, wrote in his diary, "I said good-bye with an aching heart."

The ice floe drifted into warmer

water. The men realized something terrible was happening. It was melting!

The ice under their camp began to heave and shudder. The floe started to crumble. Shackleton gave the order to launch the lifeboats.

Soon they were bobbing on the great, cold sea.

4

The Wild Ocean

The men began to row. It was bitterly cold. Huge, icy waves crashed over them. Drops of water froze on their clothes and beards.

Shackleton looked at his map. The nearest land was Elephant Island. It was very small, but it was their only chance. If they missed it, they would be swept into the open ocean.

Each night, they anchored the boats to an ice floe. Then they pitched their tents and slept on the ice.

The first night, Shackleton couldn't sleep. He got up and walked around the small camp. Suddenly a crack opened under one of the tents. He ran over.

"Somebody's missing," a man shouted.

One of the men had fallen through the crack into the icy water. Quickly, Shackleton reached down and heaved him out. The next moment, the edges of the ice crashed back together!

The men spent seven days rowing for their lives. They were tired and thirsty. Some were seasick. Painful rings of frostbite dotted their faces and hands. Their wet feet felt numb. They had to move their toes up and down to keep them from freezing.

Then it began to snow. Their clothes

froze around them. It hurt to move.
They shivered so hard that they could
hardly sleep. Many of them were
completely exhausted.

Shackleton himself barely slept. He kept watch to make sure the three little lifeboats stayed together in the stormy sea. His voice became hoarse from yelling to keep up the men's spirits.

At last the black cliffs of Elephant Island loomed before them. But where would they land? The cliffs came right down to the sea.

A strong wind began pushing the boats toward the cliffs. They were going to be dashed on the rocks!

Then someone spotted an opening in the rocks. They pulled through it. The boats came to rest on a small pebbly beach.

Shackleton and his crew fell to the ground. They were worn out, cold, and wet. But at last there was real land under their feet.

Not water. Not ice. Land!

5

Land Ho!

It was land. But Shackleton and his men would never be rescued here. No ships ever stopped at Elephant Island.

The Boss would have to go for help. Eight hundred miles away, across the stormiest ocean in the world, was South Georgia Island. There was a whaling station on the island, and

Shackleton knew that people lived there all year round.

Getting there would be dangerous. It might be impossible. But it was Shackleton's only chance to save his men. He worried about them all the time. He often dreamed that one of them had been hurt. Then he woke up screaming from his nightmares. He had to get them home.

Shackleton decided to sail for South Georgia Island in the largest of the three lifeboats. He picked five men to go with him—Captain Frank Worsley, Second Officer Tom Crean, two strong seamen, and the carpenter, who could make repairs to the boat as they sailed the rough sea. If they made it, they would get help and rescue the others.

The men said good-bye to their friends. Would they ever see each other again? No one knew. But they raised the sails and the wind swept the boat away.

The men took turns working. Huge, crashing waves filled the boat with water. Two men bailed while another man steered. The other three men lay under a low canvas deck that the ship's carpenter had built. Their sleeping bags were soaked. The reindeer skin shed so much hair that the men breathed and swallowed it. They tried to sleep, but wind and waves tossed the little boat around wildly.

One day, Shackleton saw a monster wave coming right at them. It was gigantic. "Hold on," he shouted. "It's got us!" The wave flooded the boat.

Everyone bailed furiously. Somehow, they stayed afloat.

It was a terrible journey. Ice formed on the sails and deck and made the ship heavy. Shackleton was afraid it would sink. He ordered the men to chip away all the ice they could reach.

After fifteen days, one of the men shouted, "Land ho!" Everyone stared. They could hardly believe it. Ahead of them lay the snow-covered peaks of South Georgia Island.

But before they could land, a hurricane blew up. It pushed them away, then hurled them back toward the rocky shore. The wind kept rising. Fierce waves slammed into the boat. Blinding sleet and hail made it impossible to see ahead. Shackleton wrote later, "Most of us thought the end was very near."

Shackleton and his men fought the wind and waves all night. The next day, the storm passed. The weary men pulled their battered boat onto a narrow beach.

6

Over the Glaciers

Shackleton looked around. All he saw was ice, snow, and towering mountains. The whaling station was on the other side of the island. The boat was too damaged to make it there.

The men would have to cross South Georgia Island on foot. Three of them were too weak to travel. Shackleton,

Frank Worsley, and Tom Crean would have to go by themselves.

They started climbing at daylight. When they reached a high mountain pass, they saw that there was no way down the other side. It was too steep. They went back and climbed to

another pass. Then another. Each time it was the same. If they tried to go down, they would fall to their deaths.

They climbed to the fourth pass. Night was coming on. If they didn't get down soon, they would freeze. The Boss wanted to take a chance. In front of them was a long, snowy slope. It might carry them safely to the bottom. Or it might end with a cliff. It was too dark to tell.

"Boys," Shackleton said, "if we don't go down we shall have to make a detour before we reach level going. What shall it be?"

"Try the slope," they answered.

The three men sat down, wrapped their arms and legs around each other, and off they went! They slid so fast they seemed to fly. At last they stopped in a snowbank at the bottom. They had gone a mile in just minutes. They got up and shook hands.

They walked on. Finally they saw the whaling station far below them. It was their first sight of civilization in almost eighteen months. They stared at each other in delight. Then they shook hands again.

When they reached the whaling

station, two young boys saw them first. They ran away. The three men were a terrible sight. Their hair and beards were tangled and filthy. Their faces were either black from smoke or dead white from frostbite. Their clothes hung in shreds.

They came to the station manager's house. Shackleton had met him before, but the manager didn't recognize him.

"Who are you?" the manager asked.

"My name," he said, "is Shackleton."

The manager quickly brought the three men into his house. He gave them hot baths, dry clothes, and a huge meal. Then he and his friends listened, amazed, as Shackleton told his story.

7

Rescue

Shackleton didn't waste any time. He was so worried about his crew that he couldn't rest. He had to get back to them. That night, the station manager sent a whaling ship for the three men on the other side of the island.

As soon as they were safe, the Boss set out to rescue the rest of the crew.

He borrowed a ship and sailed for Elephant Island. But he was stopped by thick ice. He had to turn around and go back.

Again and again and again, Shackleton tried to get to his men. On the last try, he was able to push through the ice. It was four months since he had left them.

But they had never given up hope. They trusted the Boss. They were sure he would save them. Every day, they packed up their belongings. They wanted to be ready when he came for them.

On August 30, 1916, someone cried, "Ship O!" All the men ran to the shore. They saw a black ship in the distance. Everyone waved and shouted.

A small boat was lowered from the ship. Slowly, it drew close. The men

saw Shackleton in the bow. They cheered loudly.

Even before he reached the shore, Shackleton started counting the men. His face was gray with fear. How many of them had lived through the terrible

months on Elephant Island?

It was for them he had sailed eight hundred miles in a tiny boat across the fierce Southern Ocean. For them, he had climbed icy mountains and glaciers to reach the whaling station. For them, he had spent months trying to break through the frozen ice around Elephant Island.

"Are you all well?" he shouted.

The men called back across the water. Shackleton's face lit up with joy at their answer.

"All well. All safe."